"A" IS FOR AIR FILTER

"B" IS FOR BRAKES

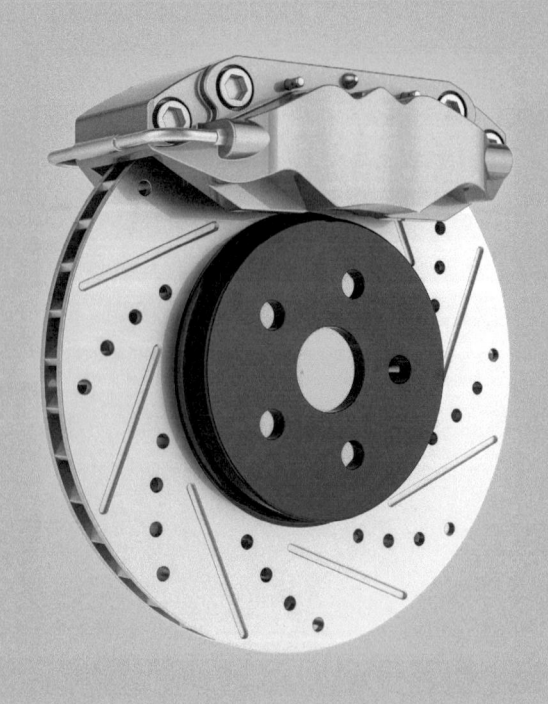

"C" IS FOR CAMSHAFT

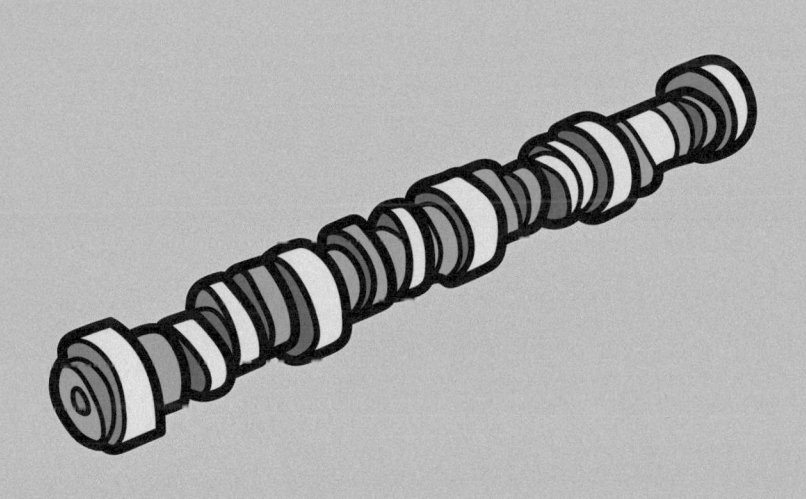

"D" IS FOR DIPSTICK

"E" IS FOR EXHAUST

"F" IS FOR FUEL PUMP

"G" IS FOR GEAR BOX

"H" IS FOR HEADERS

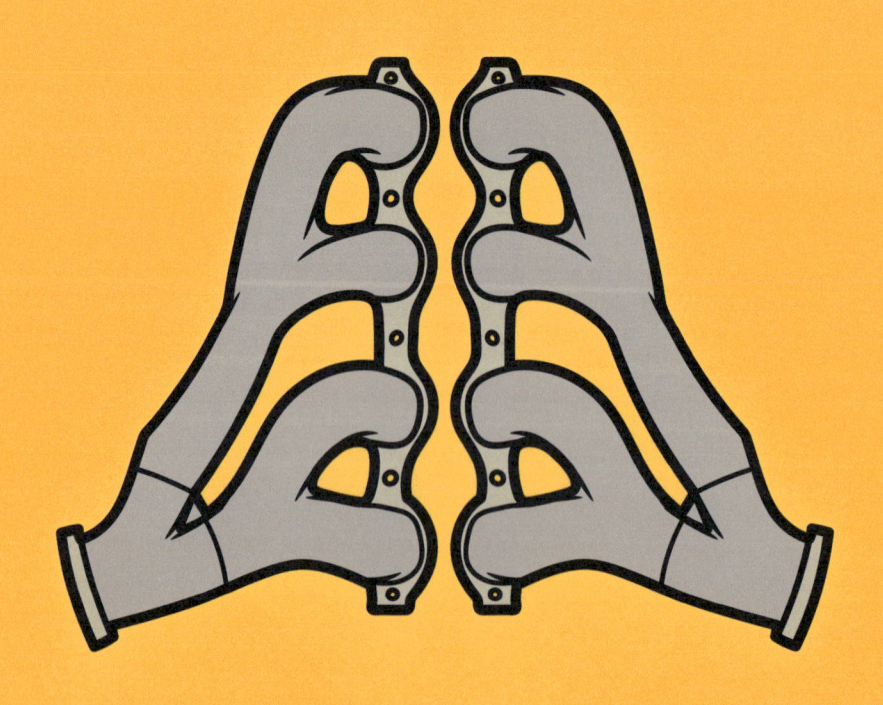

"I" IS FOR INTAKE MANIFOLD

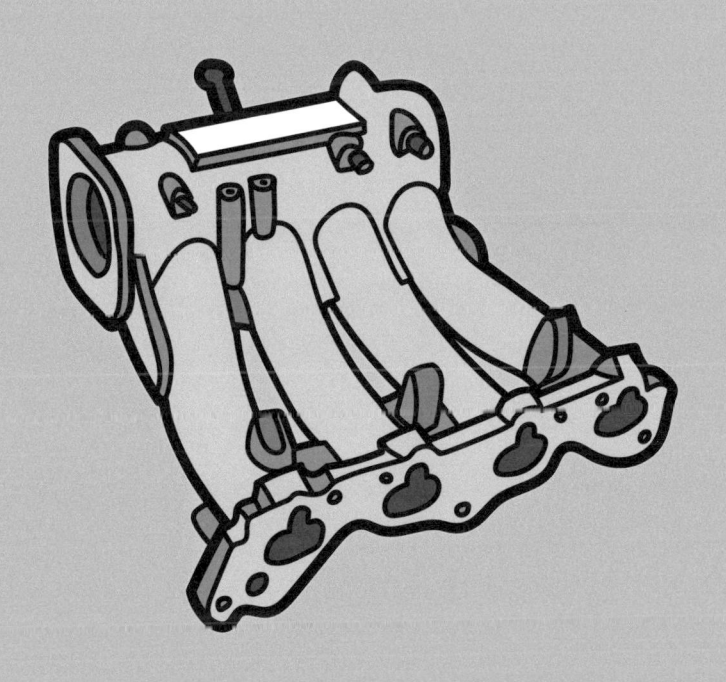

"J" IS FOR JACK

"K" IS FOR KEY

"L" IS FOR LUG NUT

"M" IS FOR MOTOR

"N" IS FOR NITROUS OXIDE

"O" IS FOR OIL CHANGE

"P" IS FOR PISTON

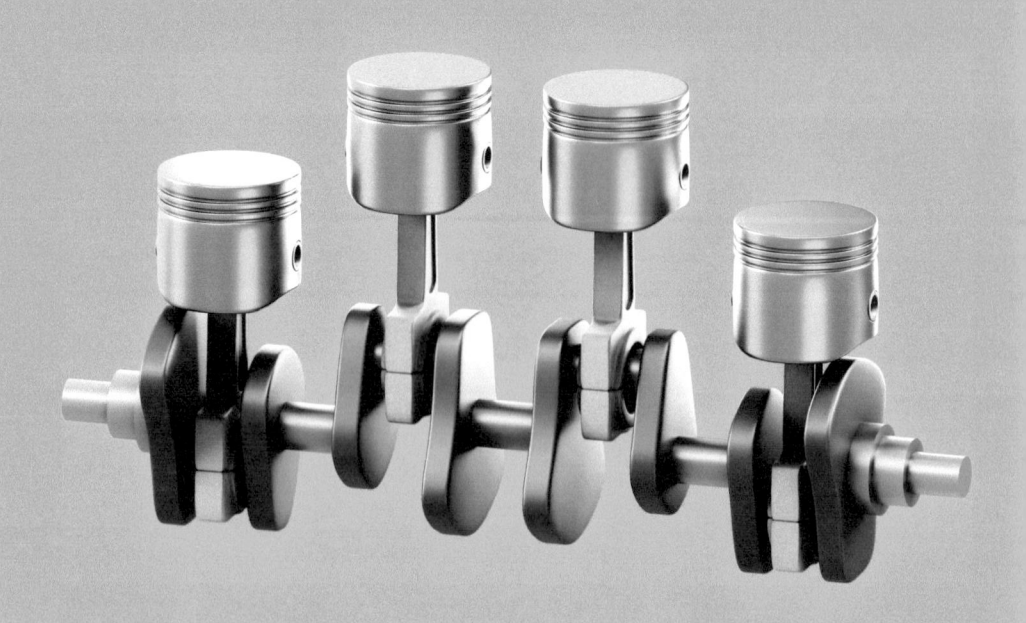

"Q" IS FOR QUICK RELEASE STEERING WHEEL

"R" IS FOR RACE CAR

"S" IS FOR SUSPENSION

"T" IS FOR TURBO

"U" IS FOR

UNDERGLOW

"V" IS FOR VALVE

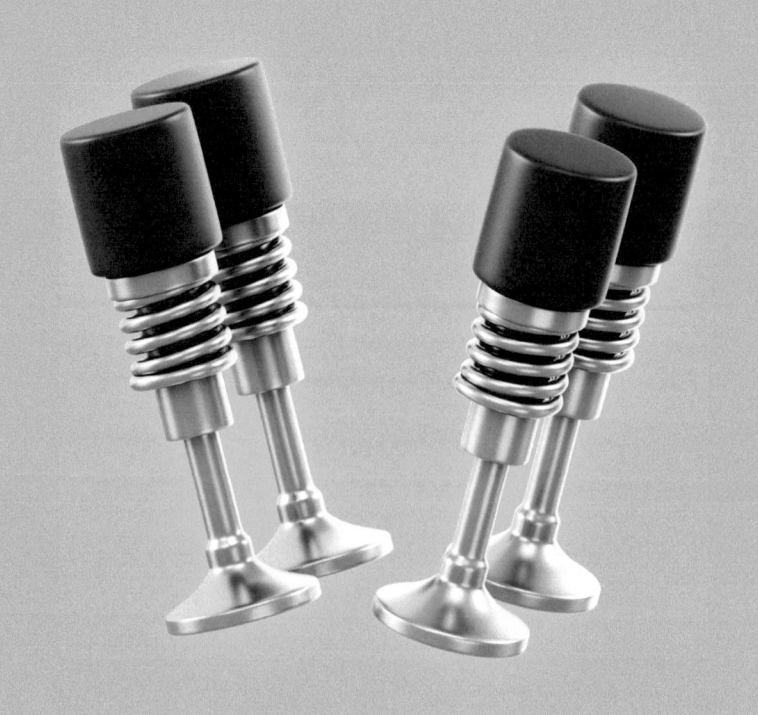

"W" IS FOR WASTEGATE

"X" IS FOR X-PIPE

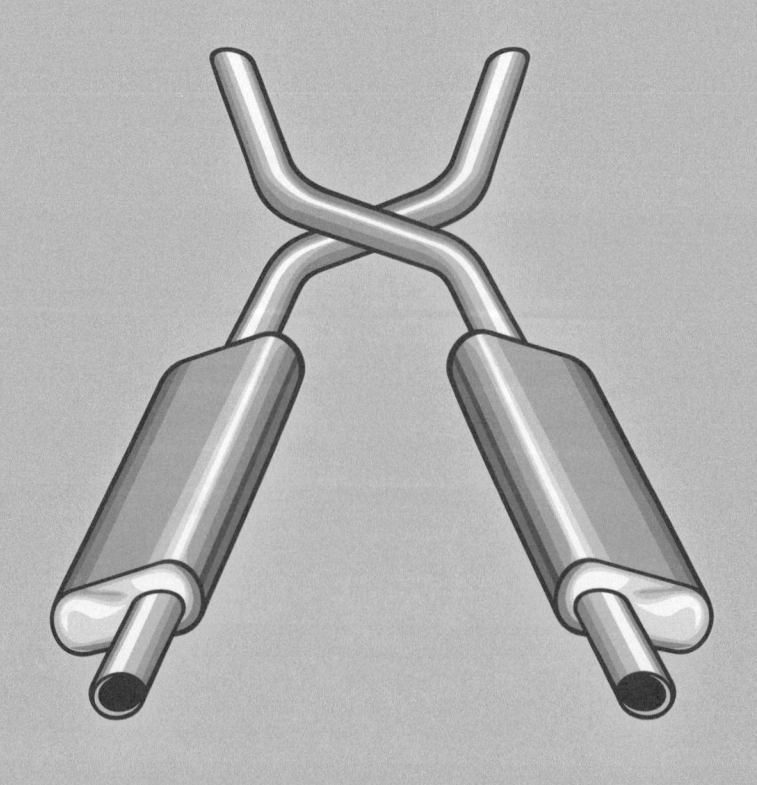

"Y" IS FOR YELLOW FLAG (CAUTION)

"Z" IS FOR ZIP TIES

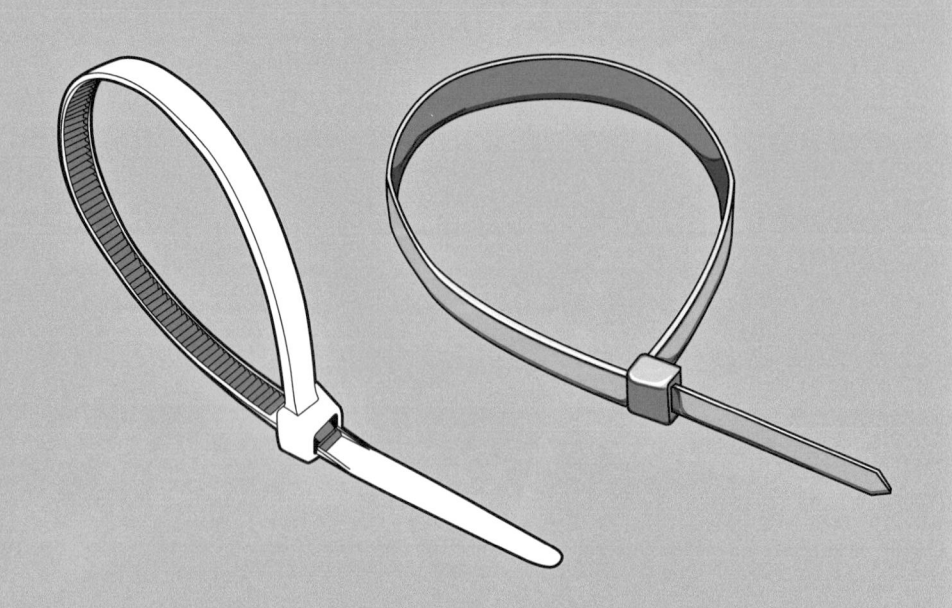